Daniel Putnam

Notes and outlines of topics in the history of education

Daniel Putnam

Notes and outlines of topics in the history of education

ISBN/EAN: 9783337215422

Printed in Europe, USA, Canada, Australia, Japan

Cover: Foto ©Paul-Georg Meister /pixelio.de

More available books at **www.hansebooks.com**

NOTES AND OUTLINES

—OF—

TOPICS

—IN THE—

HISTORY OF EDUCATION.

DANIEL PUTNAM,

Professor of Theory and Art of Teaching in Michigan State Normal School,

YPSILANTI, MICHIGAN.

THE YPSILANTIAN JOB PRINTING HOUSE.
1892.

PREFATORY NOTE.

These notes and outlines are not published, but merely printed for use in the classes studying the History of Education in the Michigan State Normal School. It has been found that such outlines save much "note-taking," and much time otherwise occupied in giving references and suggestions. The references are confined, except in a very few cases, to works accessible to students in the library of the school. Occasionally additional references are given upon special topics as they may be found of advantage.

Michigan State Normal School.
September 1, 1892.

INTRODUCTORY.

I.

The history of education, in the most comprehensive sense, is the history of civilization itself. It is a brief record of human progress and of the means and methods by which that progress has been made.

Every form of civilization has had its own peculiar education adapted to the necessities and demands of the domestic, social, civil, and religious institutions which that civilization created and in which it embodied itself. The civilization produced the education; the education conserved and perpetuated the civilization. They grew up together; the one rested upon and, at the same time, supported the other.

Oriental civilization produced an education Oriental both as to the matter of instruction and also as to systems of organization and methods of teaching. Greek civilization gave birth to Grecian education, and Roman civilization created Roman education.

One of the most important practical lessons taught by educational history, and indeed by all history, is that the education of a country, both in substance and form, in matter and spirit, in systems of organization and methods of instruction, must be in harmony with its peculiar civilization, and with the fundamental principles upon which its institutions are founded. Otherwise the condition of affairs is like that of a house divided against itself. Confusion, disaster, ruin are inevitable at no distant time.

The demand for such harmony becomes more imperative when the operations of the educational forces are directed and supervised by the civil authorities. Then movements must be in the same direction and at the same rate of speed. Modern civil and political institutions and medieval education can not travel peaceably along the same road at the same time. They look and move in opposite directions, and each claims exclusive right of way. Despotic civil government and democratic education can not exist side by side. The conflict between them is irrepressible. Free air and free thought and free speech in the school room create an imperative demand for free air, free thought, and free speech in the legislative hall and in the council chamber. Centralization in civil administration requires and justifies centralization in the organization and management of school systems; large local freedom in the one carries with it the necessity for a large measure of local freedom in the other.

These are some of the lessons which the history of education will teach, and which the student should carry with him into the school room and into the administration of educational affairs.

II.

With the usual limitations the history of education must still cover several wide and tolerably distinct provinces. The boundary lines between these can not, in some cases, be well marked or clearly defined. Nevertheless it will help to the formation of a conception of the greatness of the subject and will facilitate study to indicate, in a general way, some of these separate fields.

1. The history may treat of the general condition in respect to education of any people, or of different peoples, at some particular epoch, or during successive ages, seeking to answer questions like these: Was education provided for the people as a whole, or only for a favored few? What were the subjects of study and instruction? To what extent was instruction carried? What, in general, were the agencies and methods employed? What were the results of the education upon the character and condition of the people? What influence did the education have upon the prosperity or the decline of the nation?

2. Systems of education may be made the subjects of investigation. That is, the inquiries may be, What arrangements were made for the establishment, and support, and control of schools and other means of education? Was education under the control of the state, or of the church, or of voluntary associations, or of the family, or of individuals? Was there a connected series of schools from the lowest to the highest, or was each institution of learning an independent and isolated organism? Were permanent funds provided for the support of schools, or were they supported by local taxation, or by voluntary contributions of benevolent individuals, or by tuition fees of students?

3. Educational theories may be studied. The extent and limits of this historical field are not well defined; but investigation will concern itself with these and related inquiries: What were the purposes or ends sought by the education? Was the individual educated for his own sake, or for the sake of the community or the state? Were studies pursued for their effect in developing and disciplining the mind, or on account of their practical utility? What was the ideal of an educated man in Athens, in Sparta, among the Romans? What was the aim of the humanists, of the realists, of the naturalists? What influence has any particular type of education had upon human character and conduct? Do the lessons taught by history lead to the conclusion that education should be controlled by

the state, or by the church, or by the family? In the light of historical teaching what is practical education? The investigation of educational theories leads inevitably into the study of the philosophy of history, not of educational history merely, but of all history. It searches for causes, traces results, and from these formulates principles and rules for human conduct. In the words of Dr. H. Barnard, "The national education is at once a cause and an effect of the national character; and accordingly, the history of education affords the only ready and perfect key to the history of the human race."

4. The immediate aim may be to study the origin, the gradual development and growth of individual schools, or of particular systems of education. Of this we have examples in "The History of the Great Schools of England," in "The Schools of Charles the Great," in "The Rise and Early Constitution of Universities," and in numerous other works of similar character.

5. The history may deal chiefly and especially with the lives and labors of the great educational leaders and reformers, such men as Comenius, Pestalozzi, and Froebel, such other men as Dr. Arnold of Rugby, Horace Mann, and Mark Hopkins. In this case biography and history are combined. Educational theories are illustrated and embodied in the men, and their lives are great object lessons for their successors. This is one of the most fruitful and productive fields for educational research provided it be explored and cultivated with that wise mingling of conservatism and radicalism which bids one "examine all things and hold fast that which is good," not casting away the old simply because it bears the marks of age, nor embracing the new merely because it possesses the charm of novelty. Even reformers may sometimes prove examples for warning as well as for imitation and instruction. The experiments and mistakes of others, especially of wise and good men, should save us the expense and mortification of repeating unnecessary experiments and of making avoidable blunders.

III.

It will not be practicable or desirable to confine our study to any one of these broad fields of historical investigation. In the limited time at our command only a little beginning ean be made; a few things can be learned, and it is hoped the pathway may be discovered which will lead to greater acquisitions by future private study.

In the selection of matter for investigation regard will be had, as far as practicable, to the obvious relation between the education of previous ages and the education of the present, and to the order of evolution which has brought about the existing condition of educational affairs. The chiefest practical advantage derived from the study of any department of history is found in the light which it casts upon the institutions, the customs, the tendencies, and even the prejudices, follies, and absurdities of to-day. "If we ignore the Past we cannot understand the Present, or forecast the Future. The Radical can no more escape from the Past than the Conservative can stereotype it." The educational institutions, systems and methods of our own times can be thoroughly understood only by tracing them backward to the conditions in which they had their origin. A better acquaintance with the substance and teachings of educational history would tend to moderate somewhat the tone of self-complacent assumption which marks a portion of the educational literature of the present. Many of the principles and some of the methods of the "new education" are as old as the time of Comenius.

"In studying the Past we must give our special attention to those periods in which the course of ideas takes, as the French say, a new lead. Such a period was the Renascence."

The educational institutions and the education of the early periods of our own history as a nation were naturally fashioned mainly after the great schools of England. These schools borrowed their subjects and methods of instruction largely from the schools of the continent, and especially their humanistic curriculum from John Sturm of Strassburg. Sturm aimed to reproduce the language, and, to some extent, the education of the Augustan age of Rome, and, to a less extent, the education of Greece.

Consequently the main line of educational history, development, and progress, which most immediately concern us, has its starting point in Athens; passes with some deflections and modifications through imperial Rome; is obstructed and, at times, almost lost amid the confusions and disorders of the "Middle Ages"; reappears with some distinctness, but considerably modified by the influence of the church, for a brief time, in the reign of Charlemagne; again becomes much obscured, but reappears partially in the early Italian renascence half paganized; comes once more into view in the great upheaval of the sixteenth century.

From that period educational history takes apparently many and various directions. Movements in one direction have been met by counter movements in the opposite direction. Freedom has come into conflict with authority in subjects and methods of instruction. The church and the state have frequently made rival and irreconcilable claims to the same territory. In the realm of higher education the friends of voluntary associations and the advocates of public institutions have occasionally warned each other off as trespassers.

Humanism, realism, naturalism, have each found over-zealous advocates and partisans. Essentially the same warfare still goes on, only under new names. Out of all these conflicts real progress has been secured, and the educational institutions of to-day are the results. The history of this progress centers, as will be seen, to a large extent, in the lives, labors, and influence of a comparatively few successive reformers and leaders. These must necessarily be prominent topics of our study.

IV.

SOURCES OF INFORMATION.

1. *Direct statements* of general histories. Such statements are very few in most of the older histories. In some recent works, which give information concerning the people rather than accounts of wars and the fortunes of kings and dynasties, much valuable information can be found.

2. *Incidental allusions* in general histories, and *references* in literature to education, to educational institutions, to schools, and to teachers and their work. Such references in literary productions, until quite recently, were mostly of an amusing and humorous character, on the whole disparaging and calculated to bring the ordinary teacher into contempt. Goldsmith and Irving afford good examples.

3. *Inferences* properly drawn from the statements of historians and from literary and scientific writings. Advancement in art, science, and literature indicates advancement in education at least in some portion of the people. Books would not be written and published if there were no readers; works of art would not be produced if there were no purchasers and admirers.

4. Accounts of the explorations of the ruins of ancient cities and of the relics found among these ruins. Such accounts and relics reveal much of the civilization and consequently of the education of the peoples who built and inhabited the cities. Such explorations are being made at the present time more than ever before, and much valuable information will without doubt be obtained from them.

5. Specific histories of education generally, or histories of some department of education, and biographies of distinguished educators and teachers. Such works are not yet abundant in the English language, but are increasing. Educational essays, reviews, periodicals, and publications of various kinds afford valuable material for the student of history. This material, however, in many cases, requires very careful examination, comparison with authorities, and considerable sifting. The historian should have the impartiality and candor of a judge, and not the interested zeal of an advocate. Not a few writers, even upon educational subjects, unconsciously it may be, exhibit the spirit and temper of partisans and advocates.

The genuine student will seek information from all these sources as far as circumstances will permit.

V.

METHOD OF STUDY.

The preceding statements indicate, in a general way, the only practicable method of study. The nature of the subject, the time allotted to it, and the conditions under which the work is to be done determine this method more definitely. In its nature history is more nearly related to science than to literature. This fact must be kept in mind in the selection of a method.

Literature, as Mr. Fitch has so well said in his essay on the Renascence, consists essentially of the conceptions of an individual mind expressed in a permanent form of words. Two things are necessary to make literature: the individual conceptions and the peculiar and permanent forms of expression. The student of literature must study and master both of these. Consequently literature can be properly studied only by being read and re-read until the forms of expression are as familiar as the ideas expressed. The inquiry is not merely what an author has said, but also how did he say it.

On the other hand science is independent of any particular form of expression. It concerns itself about facts, ideas, truths, principles, and not much about the dress in which these are clothed. It only asks that facts and truths be clearly stated. The student of science seeks, in his investigations, for truth, and has little regard for words for their own sake.

In like manner the student of history is concerned about facts rather than forms of expression. He desires to learn what was said, taught, or done; what principles were enunciated, what purposes were set forth, what ideals were kept in view, what methods and means were employed, and what results were attained, rather than the language in which these things have been described. It is better that he express the facts and truths which his investigations reveal to him in words of his own selection. Consequently the reproduction *verbatim*, either orally or in note books, of extracts from encyclopedias or pages from historians, can not be regarded as a valuable exercise or a fruitful use of time or energy.

In the study of individual educational leaders and reformers the purely biographical is important only as it serves to set forth more clearly and distinctly their peculiar principles, aims, and methods. In some cases the personal fortunes of men, their characters, their principles, and their teachings are so inextricably mingled together that what they taught can be fully comprehended only when we know who and what they were in their fortunes, in their daily living, and under what conditions they "lived, and moved, and had their being." In such cases the men must be studied in order to understand their works. Their successes and failures are necessary commentaries upon their doctrines and methods of labor.

This is true in a large degree of Pestalozzi, in a less degree of Froebel, and in a still less degree of Comenius.

On the other hand, sometimes the less the personality of the man, his life and character come into view, the more weighty his utterances appear, and the more ready acceptance is given to his teachings. This is especially and most emphatically true in respect to Rousseau.

It is a common and not unnatural supposition that a man's doctrines, his peculiar principles, can be most readily gathered from a personal study of his writings. Unfortunately this supposition is not always true. Some minds, gifted above ordinary mortals, capable of giving birth to great and grand thoughts, full of high purposes and lofty aspirations, burning with holy zeal and longing to preach a new gospel to mankind, have little power to give clear expression and lucid order to their ideas. Their thoughts appear to crowd and jostle each other, and are poured forth in confusion and disorder. Such souls need interpreters. Only those who have much time and long patience can read them with profit. Some educational reformers have been of this sort. One will be wise to accept and profit by the labors of their interpreters.

Professor Laurie has prepared an admirable summary of the works of Comenius, and other writers have helped much toward a right understanding of the principles of Pestalozzi and Froebel. The student of the history of education should find opportunity, however, to read Pestalozzi's *Leonard and Gertrude* and the *Education of Man* by Froebel, as much for the sake of drinking in the spirit of the men as for becoming acquainted with their thoughts and aims. Many other books should be read, but the study of the history of education can not include, to any considerable extent, a profound study of the literature of education. The study of the literature, when possible, should supplement the study of the history. In connection with the outlines of topics in the history some books for reading will be indicated, as well as works for reference.

GENERAL REFERENCES.

Painter's History of Education.
Compayre's History of Pedagogy.
Hailman's Lectures on Pedagogy.
Browning's Educational Theories.
Shoup's History and Science of Education.
Barnard's Journal of Education.
Cyclopedia of Education and other Encyclopedias.
K. A. Schmid's Geschichte der Erziehung von Anfung an bis auf Unsere Zeit.
Buisson's Dictionnaire de Pedagogie.
Popular Science Monthly, Vols. 29, 30.

General Course in History of Education.

OUTLINES AND REFERENCES.

I.
EDUCATION IN GREECE.
1. Situation, extent, climate, etc., of Greece.
2. Origin and general character of the people.
3. Education in the heroic and early ages.

NOTE.—During the period of her prosperity and power two tolerably distinct types of education were found in Greece, one represented by Athens, the other by Sparta.

II.
ORDINARY EDUCATION AT ATHENS.
1. Solon, his laws and influence.
2. Athens in the age of Pericles. The city; the population; proportion of the people educated.
3. *Intellectual or literary education.*
(*a*) Provisions for this; relation of the State to it.
(*b*) *Childhood;* the home, mother, nurse; instruction, amusements, etc.
(*c*) *Boyhood;* Pedagogues, teachers, school rooms, school hours, discipline, studies and methods of teaching, school fees.
(*d*) *Youth;* more advanced studies, etc.
4. *Gymnastic and physical training.*
(*a*) *For boys;* Provisions for this; relation of the State to it; the palæstra and the exercises; how early this training commenced; time occupied, etc.; teachers.
(*b*) *For youth;* Gymnasia and the exercises; relation of the State to these; objects aimed at and results.
5. *Music;* vocal; instrumental; attention given to it; reasons for such study.
6. *Moral* education; character and purpose of this; relation to conduct.
7. The primary purpose or object of Athenian education; the results attained; love of the beautiful, etc.

III.

EDUCATION AT SPARTA.

1. Population; Spartans proper; other inhabitants; relation of the Spartans to these.
2. Lycurgus and his laws; their general character and influence.
3. General nature of Spartan education; relation of the State to it.
(*a*) *The child* till the age of seven; relation to the State.
(*b*) *Boyhood and Youth;* what were the schools; how managed; the teachers; treatment of the boys; subjects taught; method of teaching; moral education; music, etc.
(*c*) Objects aimed at and results attained.

IV.

EDUCATION OF WOMEN IN GREECE.

1. In heroic and early ages.
2. In Sparta.
3. In Athens.
4. Instances of highly educated women; Sappho; Aspasia and others.
5. Position of women generally.

V.

HIGHER EDUCATION IN GREECE.

1. In what it consisted chiefly; what its schools were; how instruction was given, etc.
2. *The Sophists;* who and what they were; character and teaching.
3. *Socrates* (469-399, B. C.); early life and education; personal peculiarities; subjects and method of his teaching; examples of his method; his influence; trial and death; does modern education owe anything to him? if so, what?
4. *Plato* (429-348, B. C.); education and character; connection with Socrates; his views upon education as given in the Republic and Laws; the Republic an ideal work and his education simply ideal.
5. *Aristotle* (384-322, B. C.); connection with Plato; abilities and character; connection with Alexander; school at Athens and method of teaching; his ideas upon education (Politics, Books IV, V); influence upon education in subsequent ages; Luther's opinions of him.

NOTE.—The ideal education of Plato and Aristotle was designed for the few, the aristocracy only, and not for the people as a whole. Their theories had no appreciable influence upon the education of their own times, but are of interest to us as showing the highest conceptions in respect to education of the greatest thinkers of the ancient world. Their conceptions compared with those of the present times enable us to make some estimate of the nature and direction of educational progress during the Christian centuries.

REFERENCES FOR GREEK EDUCATION.

Felton's Ancient and Modern Greece.
Becker's Charicles.
National Education in Greece in the Fourth Century B. C. by A. S. Welkins.
Aristotle by Thomas Davidson.
Barnard's Journal of Education, Vols. 14, 24.
Mahaffy's Old Greek Education.
Mahaffy's Greek Life and Thought.
Mahaffy's Social Life in Greece.
Capes' University Life in Ancient Athens.
Guhl and Koner's Life of the Greeks and Romans.
Grote's History of Greece.
Curtius' History of Greece.
Kingsley's Alexandria and her Schools.
Plato's Republic and Laws.
Aristotle's Politics.
Xenophon's Memorabilia.
Atlantic Monthly, Vol. 34.
North American Review, Vol. 14.
Atlantic Monthly, Vol. 27 (Women's Rights in Ancient Athens.)
Martin's Les Doctrines Pédagogiques des Grecs.
Chassiotis' L'Instruction Publique chez les Grecs (Paris.)

VI.
ROMAN EDUCATION.

1. Greek and Roman character compared.
2. Education in the early ages of Roman history.

(*a*) The family; position and authority of the husband and father; position of the wife and children (Hadley's Introduction to Roman Law), (John Lord's Old Roman World. Chap. 6.)

(*b*) Character of the early education; as to schools; moral education; education of girls.

3. Influence of the Greeks; changes in education; views of conservative Romans.

4. Education at the beginning of the Empire.

(*a*) Elementary schools, how established, managed and supported; discussions as to domestic and school education,

(*b*) Education of the child to the seventh year.

(*c*) From the seventh to the twelfth year; pedagogues and teachers; school regulations and discipline; studies and methods of teaching.

(*d*) After the twelfth year; secondary instruction. branches of study; the Greek language; choice of a vocation; study of the art of war; of law and politics; estimation put upon the study of oratory and eloquence; reasons for this.

(*e*) Higher education; Roman young men at Athens; subjects of study; influence upon Roman character.

5. *Quintilian* (about 40-118 A. D.); his education and character; as an advocate and teacher; his writings upon education; his plan of education, studies, methods; views as to teachers, school discipline, morals, etc.; his relation to the emperor and to education supported by the state.

6. *Plutarch* (50-138 A. D.); as a teacher and lecturer; his lives of illustrious men; his morals; essay on the training of children; influence of his writings.

7. Education taken under the patronage of the State; schools established by the early emperors; libraries established; "Romana-Hellenie Schools" (Laurie's Rise of Universities, Lecture I.)

NOTE.—The great contribution of Rome to modern civilization is not her education or her pedagogy, but Roman Law.

REFFRENCES FOR ROMAN EDUCATION.

Hadley's Introduction to Roman Law.
Merivale's History of Rome, Chapters 54, 60, 64.
Mommsen's History of Rome.
Leighton's History of Rome.
Becker's Gallus.
Quintilian's Institutes.
Plutarch's Lives, and Morals.

Life of the Greeks and Romans.
Inge's Society in Rome under the Cæsars.
Church's Roman Life in the days of Cicero.
Laurie's Rise of Universities, Lecture I.
Barnard's Journal of Education, Vols. 8, 10, 11. "Education," Vol. 4, (Wages) Vols. 5, 6.

VII.
EDUCATION DURING THE EARLY CHRISTIAN CENTURIES TO THE TIME OF CHARLEMAGNE.

1. The new principles introduced by Christianity.
2. Necessary effect of these principles upon education.
3. Social and civil condition of most of the early Christians.
4. Matter and form of the earliest education among the Christians.
5. Views of some of the "Christian Fathers" as to education, especially education of girls.
6. Pagan schools in the large centers of population during the first four centuries; (*a*) numbers and support; (*b*) studies, teaching and scholarship in these schools.
7. Relations of the Christians to these schools.
8. Causes of the decay of the Pagan schools.
9. Restrictions of the freedom of teachers and students.
10. Gradual establishment of Christian schools; kinds and character of these.

(*a*) *Catechetical* schools. The school at Alexandria.

(*b*) *Monastic* schools. (1) Difference between monasticism in the East and West; (2) some of the Western monastic orders; (3) circumstances which favored the establishment of such schools; (4) importance of these during several centuries; (5) studies taught in them, the Trivium, the Quadrivium.

(*c*) Cathedral schools. Purposes and character of these.

(*d*) Parochial schools.

11. Organization, discipline and work of Christian schools. (Laurie's Universities, Lecture 4.)
12. State of education generally on the continent during the sixth and seventh centuries.
13. Schools in Ireland and England in the sixth and seventh centuries; some of the leading teachers in these countries.

REFERENCES FOR EARLY CHRISTIAN CENTURIES.

Guizot's History of Civilization in France, Lectures 4, 8, 16, First Course.
Laurie's Rise of Universities, Lectures 1, 2, 4.
Drane's Christian Schools and Scholars.
Duruy's Later Roman Empire, Chaps. 1, 2, 3, 4, 13.

3

VIII.

PARTIAL REVIVAL OF LEARNING UNDER CHARLEMAGNE, (742-814).

1. General condition of schools and education at the beginning of his reign.

2. His own education; his character; his personal efforts for improving education, etc.

3. Alcuin (735-804); his life and work before entering the service of Charles; his work in connection with Charles; his influence upon educational affairs.

4. The school of the Palace; character of this school; the students; subjects taught; methods of instruction; learned men at the court, etc.; Rabanus Maurus.

5. Other schools established; efforts for the education of the Clergy; reform of church music; patronage of the fine arts, etc.

6. Decay of education after his death; reasons for this; state of education during the following centuries.

Note.—Some reasons for the decay and low condition of schools and education during the "Middle Ages," both before and after the time of Charles.

(*a*) The decay of the old religions and the introduction of Christianity with the resulting conflicts.

(*b*) Gradual dissolution of the Roman empire and the inroads of barbarians.

(*c*) Corruption of the Latin language, and the imperfect condition of the new languages.

(*d*) Social condition of the majority of the people, and the general confusions of the times.

(*e*) Lack of literature and books, and of the leisure and incentives for the production of these.

Whatever may have been the case subsequently, during these ages the church and the monasteries were the friends and conservators of learning.

REFERENCES FOR TIME OF CHARLEMAGNE.

Mombert's Life of Charles the Great.
Mullinger's Schools of Charles the Great.
Guizot's History of Civilization in France, Lectures 20, 21, First Course.
Drane's Christian Schools and Scholars.
Laurie's Universities, Lectures 3, 4, 5.
Barnard's Journal. Vol. 24, (Rabanus).
Duruy's History of Middle Ages, Chaps. 9, 16.
North American Review, Vol. 81, (Private Life of Charlemagne.)
Life of Alcuin by Lorenz. (London.)

IX.
FROM THE TIME OF CHARLEMAGNE TO THE REFORMATION.

1. Alfred the Great (849-901). Condition of affairs in England in his time; his own education and character; his efforts on behalf of literature and education.

2. Mohammedan schools and learning; in the East; in Spain; studies pursued; scientific progress; influence of these schools upon Christian Europe; decline of the schools.

3. Scholasticism; its essential character; influence upon independent thinking and upon intellectual and scientific progress; Abelard as a teacher and lecturer; Thomas Aquinas. (Time will allow but little attention to be given to this topic.)

4. Movements toward the close of the Middle Ages.

(*a*) Effect of the Crusades upon commerce; upon the progress of learning and schools; upon Western civilization generally.

(*b*) Education of candidates for knighthood.

(*c*) Establishment of town or Burgher schools; object of these schools and the studies taught; control of these schools.

5. Education of women during this period.

6. *Rise of Universities.*

A natural development; causes favoring and urging development; demand for specialization, etc.

7. *The Constitution and Organization.*

(*a*) The early so-called Universities not educational institutions in the modern sense; (*b*) large numbers of students gathered by the popularity of individual teachers; (*c*) some organization a necessity; (*d*) imitation of trade-guilds; "nations" organized and chiefs elected, etc.; (*e*) gradual development of organization; (*f*) "rescripts" or constitutions obtained; (*g*) essentially self-governing communities.

8. Number of students, discipline, wandering scholars, etc.

9. Privileges and immunities granted to scholars and teachers; "Benefit of clergy."

10. Faculty and "Faculties"; rise of faculties in universities, effect upon the organization; number of faculties.

11. Studies and instruction; graduation, what this was at first; titles given to teachers; the matter of "degrees," time of their institution; signification of the degrees.

12. As to buildings, libraries, apparatus, etc., of early universities; students' fees.

13. Origin and original signification of the name "college."

14. *Gerhard Groot* (1340-1384) and Brethren of the Common Life. (*a*) Aims of this organization; (*b*) character of its founder; (*c*) their schools and teaching; (*d*) general results of their labors.

REFERENCES FOR THIS PERIOD

(1) Turner's History of the Anglo-Saxons.
Knight's Popular History of England, Vol. 1.
Green's History of the English People.
Life of Alfred the Great.
North American Review, Vol. 75.
(2) Sismondi's Literature of Europe, Chap. 2.
Gibbons' Rome, Chap. 52.
Duruy's Middle Ages, Chap. 7.
(3) Hallam's Middle Ages, Chap. 9, Part II.
Drane, Chap. 12.
Student's Ecclesiastical History (Vol. 2).
Barnard's Journal, Vols. 1, 2, 4.
(6-13) Laurie's Rise of Universities.
Drane, Chap. 13.
Barnard's Journal, Vols. 1, 2, 24.
Barnard's Journal, Vol. 4.
(14) Barnard's German Teachers and Educators.

Student's Ecclesiastical History (Vol. 2).
Lacroix' Science and Literature in the Middle Ages.
Fisher's History of the Christian Church (Chap. 5).
Duruy, Chap. 23.
North American Review, Vol. 8, (Abelard).
Educational Review, March, 1891, (The Primary School in the Middle Ages).
Harper's Magazine, Vol. 43, (Schoolmasters of the Middle Ages).

X.

EARLY REVIVAL OF LEARNING IN ITALY,

1. Influence of Dante (1265-1321); of Petrarch (1304-1374); of Boccacio (1313-1375) upon the Italian language and literature, and consequently upon education.

2. Vittorino da Feltre, the great Italian teacher; early life and education; school at Padua and at Venice; school at Mantua; subjects of instruction; method of teaching; athletics or physical education; moral education; humanism.

REFERENCE FOR TOPIC X.

Symond's Revival of Learning in Italy.
Barnard's German Teachers and Educators.
Drane's Christian Schools and Scholars.
Sismondi's Literature of the South of Europe.
Barnard's Journal, Vol. 7.

Educational History from the Fifteenth Century.

XI.

FIRST PERIOD.

Effect upon learning in Western Europe of the capture of Constantinople by the Turks in 1453; results of the revival of learning in Italy; results in Germany; conflicts between the friends of the old order of things and the advocates of the new learning; general condition of the monastic and other schools.

XII.

Note.—The history of educational progress for several centuries consists mainly of an account of the lives, labors, principles, and methods employed by eminent individual leaders and reformers. Only the most eminent of these can be specially studied. They are divided by some writers into Humanists, Realists, and Naturalists. The division is convenient as marking the steps of the inevitable progress of the human mind from servitude to freedom, and from the study of words to the study of things.

1. AGRICOLA (1443-1485), called sometimes the father of German humanism. Brief sketch of his life; his opinion of the schools of his time; of studies and method; his most important service to education.
2. REUCHLIN (1455-1522), "the father of modern Hebrew studies." Life and education; writings; study of Hebrew; controversies; general results of his labors.
3. ERASMUS (1467-1536). Education and scholarship; educational writings; studies which he advocated; influence upon learning and education; his Greek testament; estimate of him as a man.
4. LUTHER (1483-1546). Brief sketch of his life and education; views as to the training of children; duties of parents; as to schools; studies and methods; importance of education to the state; compulsory education; as to teachers and teaching; his translation of the Bible; influence generally upon education in Germany.
5. MELANCHTHON (1497-1560). His education and character; his relation to Luther; his work as a teacher; his text-books; his work for school

systems; grouping or grading pupils; influence upon education and learning.

6. JOHN STURM (1507-1589). His early educational work; his school and work at Strasburg; his ideal of education; the organization of his school and his graded course of study; the excellencies and defects of his system; his influence upon the education of his own and of subsequent times.

Note.—Sturm's curriculum of studies was narrow and, according to modern standards, seriously defective. But he evidently did more to give form to the humanistic education than any other man of that age—a form which it retained almost to our own age.

7. SCHOOLS OF THE JESUITS.

Sketch of the founder of the order, Ignatius Loyola (1491-1556); their system of education (*Ratio Studiorum*); preparation of teachers; organization of schools, lower and higher; classes of pupils; courses of studies; of studies; officers and teachers and supervision; methods of instruction; use of emulation; discipline of the schools; examinations; daily order of work; moral and religious training; object aimed at in their system of education.

Progress of the order in its early history; extent of its educational work; estimate put upon the Jesuit schools and education by various writers.

Note.—To this time education had been almost exclusively humanistic. The main subject of study was the Latin language, some attention being given to Greek. The "mother tongue" was generally treated with neglect. The period of reaction, however, was beginning. "Verbal realism" came first and prepared the way for realism proper, that is, for the study of things themselves rather than the study of descriptions of things.

REFERENCES FOR FIRST PERIOD.

Quick's Educational Reformers.
Barnard's German Teachers and Educators.
Farrar's Essays on a Liberal Education, Lecture I.
Painter's Luther on Education.
Hughes' Loyola and the Educational System of the Jesuits.
Barnard's Journal of Education, Vol. 14.
D'Aubigné's History of the Reformation.
Laurie's Introduction to Life of Comenius.
Education, Vol. I. Vol. 10 (Sturm).

XIII.
SECOND PERIOD.

Note.—Some writers, whose opinions are entitled to great respect, reckon among the earliest educational reformers of the realistic or naturalistic school, FRANÇOIS RABELAIS (1483-1553), basing his claims to such a place upon his "Life of Gargantua" and "Heroic Deeds of Pantagruel." Even these writers, however, admit that his works are not "suited for the reading of ordinary students." One may be pardoned for doubting whether his influence upon educational progress has been appreciable. (See Browning, Quick, and Compayré.)

1. MONTAIGNE (1533-1592). His own education; his educational views found chiefly in his essays upon Pedantry and upon the Education of Children; some of his thoughts; studies recommended; methods of education; how one should read; views upon the education of women; his influence upon education not great.

2. ASCHAM, ROGER (1515-1568). His own education; work as a teacher; relation to Elizabeth; occasion for writing the "Scholemaster;" character and purpose of that work; method of teaching Latin; his contribution to educational progress.

Note.—For some information concerning Richard Mulcaster see Quick.

3. BACON, LORD FRANCIS (1561-1626). His education and character; essays; aim of his "Advancement of Learning"; methods of seeking after truth; his especial contribution to the progress of education.

4. RATICH or RATKE (1571-1635). His own education; education of the young should begin with the mother-tongue; what he claimed to be able to do; experiments and failures; methods of teaching reading; method in Latin; comparison of his method and Asham's; his educational principles; what credit should be given him; relation to Comenius.

REFERENCES FOR XIII.

Quick's Educational Reformers.
Barnard's Journal, Vols. 3, 4, 5, 11, 13.
Barnard's German Teachers and Educators.
Ascham's Scholemaster.
Introduction to Laurie's Life of Comenius.
Gill's System's of Education (Ascham).
Barnard's English Pedagogy.
Montaigne on Education by MacAlister.

XIV.

COMENIUS, JOHN AMOS (1592-1671).

(*a*) Condition of Europe during his life-time ; his education ; religious connection and character ; rector of school at Prerau and work there ; labors at Fulneck ; wanderings ; work at Lesna ; visit to England ; visit to Sweden and residence at Elbing, and work there ; return to Lesna and school at Patak ; final residence at Amsterdam and death.

(*b*) His educational writings ; the Great Didactic and some of its most characteristic teachings and principles ; general aim of education ; method of education under the heads *surely, easily, solidly ;* some practical problems in school work ; method in teaching languages, the four steps ; morality and piety ; school discipline ; practical hints to teachers.

(*c*) His proposed school system, four periods and four grades of schools ; the organization and work of each school.

(*d*) In respect to the teaching of Latin ; criticism on the prevailing method ; suggestions as to reform of method.

(*e*) His text-books ; practically only the *Janua Linguarum* in various forms ; *The Vestibulum* (Latin Primer) ; *The Janua* proper ; *The Atrium*. The best known and most popular work, *The Orbis Pictus*.

(*f*) Write an epitome of his most important and characteristic educational principles and teachings.

Note.—Most of the fundamental principles and maxims of the so-called "New Education" are found in the writings of Comenius. He is justly entitled to rank among the world's greatest educational reformers.

REFERENCES FOR THE STUDY OF COMENIUS.

Laurie's Life of Comenius.
Quick's Educational Reformers.
Painter ; Compayré ; Browning ; Barnard's Journal, Vol. 5.
Barnard's German Teachers and Educators.
Educational Review for March, 1892.

XV.

1. MILTON, JOHN (1608-1674). His definition of education; his "Captractate"; proposition for the erection of an agricultural college; scheme of education, its value.

1. LOCKE, JOHN (1632-1704). His profession; "Thoughts upon the Education of Children"; physical education; manual labor; home education; requisites in a teacher; influence of education; estimation of "learning"; study of languages; travel; general aim of education; discipline, rewards, punishments; Locke's ideal an English gentleman.

3. FRANKÉ, AUGUSTUS HERMAN (1663-1727). His own education; infant school at Hamburg; beginning of his work at Halle; building of the orphan-house; rules as to discipline, etc.; sources of income; growth of his institutions; extent of the various departments; mission work; probable influence of the institutions at Halle upon benevolent and reformatory work in subsequeut times.

4. ROUSSEAU, JEAN JAQUES (1712-1778). His personal character; made famous by an essay on the evils of civilization; the artificial life and society of his time; his "Émile" contains his ideas on education; general outline of the work; Émile during the first twelve years, education of the senses; from twelve to fifteen, intellectual education; the affections, moral and religious education; ideas upon the education of women; influence attributed to the Émile.

Note.—Rousseau and the Émile have been extravagantly praised. The Émile has real value and could not well be spared from educational literature, but its value has been over-estimated. An education according to nature is advocated, but Émile is a purely imaginary being placed in the most unnatural and impossible conditions. Rousseau did good work in destroying; made in fact "a clean sweep," but in building up he did little or nothing.

BASEDOW, JOHANN BERNHARD (1723-1790). His education and character; description by Goethe; disciple of Rousseau; substance and form of his "Elementary" book; "Book of Methods"; his school, "Philanthropinum" at Dessau; subjects and methods of instruction; method in teaching languages; the "examination"; expectations and disappointment; influence of this experiment upon schools and education; in what respect an imitator of Comenius; in what respects an anticipation of some modern ideas and methods.

REFERENCES FOR XV.

Quick's Educational Reformers.
Barnard's German Teachers and Educators.
Barnard's English Pedagogy.
Barnard's Journal, Vols. 2, 5, 6, 8, 11, 13, 20, 26.
Milton's "Tractate" on Education.

Locke's Thoughts on Education.
Morley's Rousseau, (London).
Rousseau's Emile.
Painter ; Compayré ; Browning.
Laurie's Addresses (Milton).
Leitch's Practical Educationists (Locke).
Gill's Systems of Education (Milton, Locke).

XVI.

PESTALOZZI, JOHN HENRY (1746-1827).
1. Parentage ; early education ; peculiarities.
2. Student life at Zurich ; the times.
3. Experiment in Agriculture ; failure.
4. Experiments in the education of his own child ; influence of Rousseau.
5. Experiment in the school for poor children at Neuhof ; failure.
6. Life from 1780 to 1798 ; disturbed condition of the country ; his writings ; Evening Hour of a Hermit ; Leonard and Gertrude.
7. Work at Stanz ; causes of failure.
8. Work at Burgdorf; school in the castle; Krüse; books and methods.
9. Institute at Yverdun ; assistants ; character of the work done ; physical training ; patronage and success ; influence of the institute.
10. Decline of the institute and last years of Pestalozzi.
11. Character of Pestalozzi ; source of his power.
12. His educational principles ; their application in elementary instruction ; comparison with Comenius ; Pestalozzi's influence upon educational progress and upon methods of instruction.

REFERENCES FOR STUDY OF PESTALOZZI.

De Guimp's Life and Work of Pestalozzi.
Krüse's Life and Work of Pestalozzi.
Quick's Educational Reformers.
Joseph Payne's Lectures.
Barnard's Pestalozzi and Pestalozzianism.
Painter ; Compayré ; Browning ; Hailman.
Barnard's Journal, Vols. 3, 4, 5, 7.
Leitch's Practical Educationists.
Gill's Systems of Education.
Education, Vols. 3, 11.
W. T. Harris' Reports of St. Louis Schools, 1867-8.
Leonard and Gertrude, translated by Eva Channing.

XVII.

FROEBEL, FRIEDRICH (1783-1852).
Early life and education; various employments and experiences; first work in teaching; with Pestalozzi at Yverdun; subsequent experiences and labors; opens a school at Griesheim, removed to Keilhau; character of the school; publication of "*The Education of Man*"; experinces in Switzerland; school at Burgdorf; attention turned to the condition of children before school age; first Kindergarten opened; further labors; Baroness von Marenholtz-Bulow; female teachers; establishment of Kindergartens forbidden in Germany; end of Froebel's life; his character.

Froebel's idea of the aim of education; Quick's judgment of the character of his writings; development through self-activity; the essential difference between Froebel and Pestalozzi; real nature and character of the Kindergarten; danger of mere mechanism; importance of the inspiring idea; what the "New education" is; influence of the Kindergarten spirit and methods upon the management and instruction of primary schools; a statement of the characteristic principles of Froebel; a comparison of Comenius, Pestalozzi, and Froebel.

REFERENCES FOR THE STUDY OF FROEBEL.
Froebel's Education of Man, translated by Hailman.
Hailman's Kindergarten Culture.
Reminiscences of Froebel, translated by Miss Peabody.
Miss Peabody's Lectures to Kindergartners.
Barnard's Papers on the Kindergarten.
Joseph Payne's Lectures.
Marwedel's Child Nature and Kindergarten.
Sherriff's Essays and Lectures on the Kindergarten.
Quick's Educational Reformers
Barnard's Journal, Vol. 30.
Painter; Compayré.
Education, Vol. 3.

XVIII.

SOME SPECIAL SYSTEMS AND METHODS.

1. *The Monitorial System.*

(A) BELL, ANDREW (1753-1832).

Superintendent of Orphan school at Madras, India; difficulties and experiments; use of sand; pupil teachers employed; success; account published in England; high estimate of the value of the system; controversy with Lancaster; formation of the "National Society" by members of the established church; subsequent great work of the society.

(B) LANCASTER, JOSEPH (1778-1838).

His first school; why pupil-teachers were first employed; success of his school; development of the monitorial system; formation of the British and Foreign School Society by dissentors; work of the society and success of the system; Lancaster in America; monitorial schools in New York estimate put upon the system by DeWitt Clinton and others; speedy decline of the system.

Conditions in England and in New York which favored the adoption of the Monitorial system; the good accomplished; reasons for its decline; lessons taught by the history of the system.

REFERENCES ON THE MONITORIAL SYSTEM.

Southey's Life of Dr. Bell.
Randall's Common School System of New York.
North American Review, Vol. 18.
Barnard's Journal, Vol. 10.
Leitch's Practical Educationists.
Education, Vol. 1. Compayré.
Gill's Systems of Education.
Bell's Elements of Tuition (London, 1815).
Lancaster's British System of Education (London, 1810).
Meiklejohn's Dr. Andrew Bell (London).

2. METHOD AND DOCTRINES OF JACOTOT, JOSEPH (1770-1840).

His method of instruction at Dijou; his method at Louvain; conclusions and generalizations from this experiment, his "paradoxes"; meaning and application of "All is in all"; application to "Télémaque" in learning French; his directions; teaching of reading, writing, etc., by his method; what is valuable in his method and doctrine; his method compared with Ascham's.

REFERENCES FOR JACOTOT.

Joseph Payne's Lectures.
Quick's Educational Reformers.

Jacotot's Enseignement Universel, (Paris).

Jacotot et sa méthode d' émancipation intellectuelle, by Barnard Perez, (Paris, 1883).

3. HAMILTON, JAMES ((1775-1829).

How he learned the French language ; his method described ; success as a teacher both in America and England ; books published ; popularity of the method for a time ; points of resemblance to Ascham's method.

See Barnard's Journal, Vol. 6, (Methods of Teaching Latin, etc.)

Edinburg Review, Vol. 44, (Hamilton's System).

History of the Hamiltonian System, (London, 1831).

Note 1.—When time permits this topic may be pursued at greater length with much profit. A careful study of methods which have, by force of circumstances, attained a temporary popularity in the past affords an instructive lesson for the present. Not a few of the "new" things of to-day are old things somewhat modified and occasionally, but not always, improved. They are, however, neither the better nor the worse for being revivals of olden times.

Note 2.—Some persons and some topics have been omitted in these outlines of the general course in the History of Education on account of the necessary limitation of the work. Others have been omitted because they belong more properly among the educational discussions and doctrines of the day than in the domain of history. Among these are the works of Herbert Spencer and Alexander Bain which are worthy of careful and discriminating study.

Note 3.—The general course is supplemented by special courses treating of the history and present condition of education in the United States, and of the present educational condition and systems of other countries, especially of England, Germany and France.

SPECIAL COURSE.

EDUCATION IN THE UNITED STATES.

Note.—Boone's excellent History of Education in the United States is taken as a general guide in this subject.

I.

COLONIAL PERIOD.

1. *Early schools* in (a) New England ; (b) in New York ; (c) in other colonies ; how established and supported.
2. *School systems and laws* in the colonies.
(a) Law of 1647 in Massachusetts.
(b) Law of 1650 in Connecticut.
(c) In New York and other colonies.
3. *Management and support of schools;* extent of studies and instruction ; school books ; qualifications and salaries of teachers ; discipline, etc.
4. *Colonial Colleges.*
(a) Harvard, and John Harvard.
(b) William and Mary.
(c) Yale, and Elihu Yale.
(d) Princeton, (College of N. J.)
(e) University of Pennsylvania and Philadelphia Academy.
(f) Columbia (King's).
(g) Brown (R. I. College).
(h) Dartmouth, and Dr. Wheelock.
(i) Rutgers (Queens).

REFERENCES.

Boone's History of Education in the United States.
Elliott's History of New England, Chap. 46.
McMaster's History, Vol. I, Chap. 1.
Barnes' Centenary History, Chap. 4.
Palfrey's New England, Vol. II, Chap. 1.
Weeden's History of New England.

Colonial History of New York.
Randall's History of Common School System of New York.
Brodhead's History of New York, Vol. I.
Robert's History of New York.
Dunshu's School of the Dutch Church.
Sypher's School History of Pennsylvania, Chap. 36.
Stockwell's History of Education in Rhode Island.
Neill's Vetusta Virginia.
Lodge's English Colonies in America.
Thomas's History of Printing.
E. Everett's Oration's, Vol. I. p. 173.
Lowell Institute Lectures, 1869, p. 351.
Yale Review, 1885, Yale Lit. Magazine.
North American Review, Vol. 122, p. 191 ; 47, p. 274.
Barnard's Journal, Vol. 1, 4, 5, 7, and others, (See Index.)
Atlantic Monthly, Jan. 1885, (Dames School).
Education, Vol. I, p. 297.
De Bow's Review, Vol. 20.
Romage's Local Government and Free Schools in S. C.
Report of U. S. Commissioner of Education, 1875,(old ideas of education etc.) pp. vii-xxiv.
 Adams' College of William and Mary (Bureau of Education).
 Adams' Jefferson and the University of Virginia (Bureau of Education).
 Bush's Higher Education in Massachusetts, (Bureau of Education).
 Histories of Harvard University.
 Histories of Yale College.
 Histories of Darmouth College.
 Histories of Columbia College.
 Histories of Brown University.
 Histories of Princeton College, and Log College.
 Educational Review, April and June, 1892.
 Colonial Education in South Carolina, Appendix II in History of Higher Education in South Carolina.

II.

TRANSITION PERIOD, 1775-1825.

 1. Ideas in the country generally in respect to public common schools.
 2. Influence of this general public sentiment upon the schools.
 3. Character and condition of the common schools generally during this period ; support of the schools ; school fees and rate bills ; studies and text-books ; school houses, apparatus, etc.
 4. Teachers of the common schools generally, qualifications, social position, etc.
 5. Education provided for girls.

6. Academies and other secondary schools ; conditions favoring their establishment ; studies and instruction in these ; relation to the colleges ; how supported and managed. Phillip's Exeter Academy in New Hampshire ; Phillips Andover Academy in Massachusetts ; Boston Latin School, etc.

7. Higher institutions of learning, colleges and professional schools, during this period ; general character of these schools.

Note.—For a view of society in the early years of the present century, see Schouler's History of the United States, Vols. II, III ; Coffin's Building the Nation, etc.

REFERENCES.

Many of the works named under the previous topic.
McMaster, Vol. II, Chap. 7.
Adams' Free Schools of United States.
Social Life in the Colonies.
Coffin's Building of the Nation, Chap. 5.
Barnard's Journal, Vols. 5, 12, (Girls), 6, 7, 12, 13, 16, 30, and some others, (See Index).
Putnam's Pamphlet Summary.
First Constitutions of the States.
New Englander, January, 1885 (Academies).

III.

THIRD PERIOD, FROM ABOUT 1825 TO THE PRESENT TIME.

REVIVAL OF INTEREST in the common schools about 1837.

(a) Labors of Horace Mann and his associates in Massachusetts.

(b) Labors of Henry Barnard and others in Connecticut and Rhode Island.

(c) Interest in New York and in other States.

(d) Some prominent educators and friends of education of that time, besides Mr. Mann and Mr. Barnard, and their work.

Note.—Educational effort and progress have been along several tolerably distinct lines, and the results can be best ascertained and estimated by considering briefly in turn some of the most important of these lines.

SCHOOL SYSTEMS, ORGANIZATIONS AND SUPERVISION.

(a) *The Single District System.* Conditions which created and perpetuated this system in New England ; its adoption in New York and other States ; advantages and disadvantages of this system.

(b) *Town or Township System.* The original system in New England ; influences which have caused its re-adoption there; adoption in other States ; advantages and disadvantages of this system.

(c) *The County* as the unit of control and supervision. Why readily adopted in some States and not in others ; advantages and disadvantages of this system.

(d) *City Supervision;* methods by which this is administered ; school boards, committees, and superintendents, etc.

(e) *State Supervision* and control. Growth of the idea of such supervision ; modes of administration, boards of education, State superintendents ; powers exercised by these officers.

2. PROVISION FOR THE SUPPORT OF SCHOOLS.

(A.) *Temporary and local provision.*

The early schools were generally supported by income from tuition fees or rate bills, by donations from benevolent individuals of land or other property and by local taxation or grants of land by towns or other municipal bodies.

(B.) *Beginnings of permanent funds.*

(a) Donations by individuals of funds for the establishment of Academies and higher institutions.

(b) Appropriations of land and other property by State legislatures ; such action in Massachusetts, Connecticut, New York, and some other States ; lotteries authorized.

(C.) *Congressional Land-grants, etc.*

Provisions of the ordinance of 1787 ; section 16 ; townships and other lands granted for upport of colleges, etc.; section 36 added ; swamp and saline lands ; distribution of surplus revenue in 1836 ; grant for agricultural colleges, etc.; permanent educational funds of different States ; control and management of these funds.

3. *Studies and Instruction,* compared with the studies and instruction of fifty and one hundred years ago.

(a) The Elementary and Common Schools.

(b) The High and other secondary schools.

(c) Universities, colleges, and other institutions of advanced learning.

(d) Directions in which changes have been most marked in schools of different grades ; tendency of the present time as to changes.

REFERENCES.

Reports of the U. S. Commissioners of Education and circulars of information. (See Index in Report for 1888-89.

Educational Reports and School Laws of the different States.

Proceedings of the National Educational Association and of other similar associations.

Life and Works of Horace Mann.

School Supervision by J. L. Pickard.'

School Supervision by W. H. Payne.

City School Systems of the United States by J. D. Philbrick (Bureau o Education, Circular I, 1885).

Adams' Free Schools of the United States.
History of Land Grants in the Northwest Territory by G. W. Knight.
History of Federal and State Aid to Higher Education by F. W. Blackmar, (Bureau of Education).
The whole series of "Contributions to American Educational History" published by the Bureau of Education.
American State Universities by Ten Brook.
North American Review, Vol. 13, (Public Lands for Public Schools).
Education, Feb., 1887, (Ordinance of 1787).
Barnard's Journal, Vol. 5, (Horace Mann); Vol. 1, (Common Schools in Connecticut); Vol. 4, (Western Reserve school fund).
(See Index of Journal for other references).

Note.—See Indexes to Magazines and other periodicals, especially those devoted to education. The Bibliography of Boone's History will be of great service.

Crasby's Teaching in Three Continents,
Fitch's Notes on American Schools.

IV.

SCHOOLS AND OTHER MEANS FOR THE PREPARATION OF TEACHERS.

1. NORMAL SCHOOLS.

(A.) *In Europe.* Early history; the Abbé de la Salle at Rheims, 1681; 'The Christian Brothers" and their work; Franké at Halle, 1697; J. J. Hecker at Stettin, 1735, at Berlin, 1748. Berlin school removed to Potsdam, a short distance from Berlin, where it still exists. Establishment of these schools in various parts of Europe; Normal Schools in Prussia at the present time, number, organization, studies and instruction; Normal Schools in France, organization, etc.

(B.) *In the United States.* Early history.

(a) In Massachusetts. Labors of James G. Carter, Charles Brooks, Edmund Dwight, Horace Mann and others in Massachusetts, 1830-1837; S. N. Hall at Concord, N. H., 1823, and subsequent labors of Mr. Hall; opening of the Normal School at Lexington, July 3, 1839; at Barre, Sept. 4, 1839, and at Bridgewater, Sept. 9, 1840; studies and instruction in these schools; opposition encountered; other Normal Schools in Massachusetts.

(b) In New York. DeWitt Clinton's recommendations, 1826; memorial to Legislature, 1830; continued efforts for the establishment of a Normal School; academical departments for the education of teachers; Normal School opened at Albany, 1844; schools subsequently established in New York.

(c) In other States. Normal School for girls in Philadelphia, 1848;

Normal School at New Britain, Conn., 1849; at Ypsilanti, Mich., Oct. 5, 1852; Schools in other places soon after.

(C.) Normal Schools in the United States at the present time ; State ; city ; private ; purposes of these schools ; organization ; different grades ; courses of studies and instruction ; training or practice departments; model schools ; criticisms upon normal schools ; advantages afforded by these schools.

2. TEACHERS' INSTITUTES. Early history of such institutes ; conflicting claims as to the first institutes ; one claimed at Hartford, Conn., 1839; first in New York at Ithaca, 1843 ; general character of the early institutes ; organization and management of institutes at present in different States ; their value and their defects.

Note.—Among other means for preparing teachers for their work, which can not be considered at length here, are Professorships of the Theory and Art of Teaching and courses of lectures upon Pedagogics rnd Pedagogy, in many of the Universities and Colleges, teachers' associations, national, state and local, and many excellent books, periodicals, and papers devoted to the discussion of educational affairs.

REFERENCES.

Barnard's Journal, (See Index).
Barnard's Normal Schools.
Randall's History of Common School System of New York.
Fifty-Third Annual Report of the Massachusetts Board of Education, 1888-89.
State Educational Reports and Laws.
Prussian Schools through American eyes.
French Schools through American eyes.
Reports of United States Commissioner of Education.
Proceedings of National Educational Association.
Educational Reviews and periodicals.
Klemm's European Schools.
Payne's Contributions to the Science of Education.

V.

EDUCATION OF WOMEN.

1. Education of girls in the Colonial period and during the first years of the present century.
2. Early efforts for improving the education of women. Experiment in Boston and the result ; schools for girls opened in various places ; public sentiment upon the education of women.
3. Efforts and labors of individuals.
(a) Mrs. Emma Hart Willard and her educational work.

(b) Miss Catherine E. Beecher and her labors.
(c) Mary Lyon and Mount Holyoke (1837).
4. Institutions exclusively for the higher education of women recently established.
(a) Elmira Female College (1855).
(b) Vassar College, opened 1866; sketch of the institution and its work.
(c) Wellesley College, Wellesley, Mass., opened 1875; its history, character, and work.
(d) Wells College, Aurora, N. Y., (1868).
(e) Smith College, Northampton, Mass., (1875) ; its founder, its rank, and work.
(f) Bryn Mawr College, Bryn Mawr, Pennsylvania (1885); its character and work.
5. Co-educational institutions of a high rank. These are now very numerous, especially in the West; some of the most important to be noticed.
6. "Annex" at Harvard university; privileges at Yale university and at other advanced institutions.
7. Estimate of the advance in the education of women in the United States within fifty years ; public sentiment upon the subject ; women in the "Professions," physicians, etc.

EDUCATION OF WOMEN IN EUROPE.

(a) *In England;* experiment at Hitchin near Cambridge (1869); Girton College (1873); Newnham College at Cambridge ; Lady Margaret Hall and Sommerville Hall at Oxford ; London university opened to women (1878); other colleges established; Royal Holloway College in Egham ; public sentiment in England.

(b) In other European countries; France, Switzerland, Sweden, Denmark, etc.; condition in Germany ; public sentiment in Germany.

REFERENCES.

Previous references to Reports and other public documents.
Barnard's Journal (See Index).
Vol. 6, (Mrs. Willard); Vol. 13, (Girls in Boston) ; Vol. 10, (Mary Lyon); Vol. 28, (Catherine Beecher); Vol. 11, (Vassar); Vol. 30, (Wellesley); Vol. 27, (Smith College).
Bush's Higher Education in Massachusetts.
(Mount Holyoke, Wellesley, Smith.)
"Education," Vol. 5 (Mary Lyon), Vol 6, (education for girls), Vols. 7, 8, (colleges for women), Vol. 10, (women in England).
"Academy," Vol. 2, (Bryn Mawr).
Atlantic Monthly, Vol. 3, (ought women to learn the alphabet).
North American Review, Vol. 118.
Popular Science Monthly, Dec. 1886, (Higher education of women, adverse).

Life of Mary Lyon.
Brackett's Education of American girls.
Dall's College, Market, and Court.
Barnard's Female Schools and Education.
Orton's Liberal Education of Women.
Shirreff's Intellectual Education for Women.
Lange's Higher Education of Women.
Klemm's European Schools.
Catalogs and circulars of the Colleges.

www.ingramcontent.com/pod-product-compliance
Lightning Source LLC
Chambersburg PA
CBHW020150170426
43199CB00010B/977